THE GREATER GOOD

A MUST READ FOR ANYONE IN PUBLIC SERVICE. AN INSPIRING READ FOR EVERYONE ELSE

CHITTARANJAN SAMAJPATI

To the memory of my parents, to my family and to the
people I served

Contents

Contents

Preface

This book is the outcome of a conflict - that between my inherent aversion to the public spotlight, and my desire to bring alive the many opportunities and challenges of public service. And I am glad that the latter ultimately emerged victorious.

In these pages, I have tried to cover a wide spectrum of episodes including interactions with the Prime Minister, principled battles with Chief Ministers and Ministers as well as with noted business houses, taking charge during natural calamities such as floods, maintaining law and order in trying times, impacting public health and education and many more. There is also a sprinkling of short, lighter anecdotes in the line of duty.

My hope is that the stories in this book will encourage some of you, my readers, to commit to the greater good, albeit with your eyes wide open. And for the rest of you who are in positions of leadership, I expect there to be little takeaways that you will find worthwhile.

Acknowledgements

My family for their understanding and their unflinching support during my years in service, and thereafter for providing the necessary nudges to bring this book into being.

EPISODES (Chapters I-XIV)

Fascinating stories with a fair bit of detail and texture

CHAPTER I

A Prophecy

Deputy Secretary, Industries, Ahmedabad

Ahmedabad, with its numerous textile mills, used to be called the Manchester of India. Just like its British counterpart, with its river Mersey, the city was situated on the bank of the river Sabarmati. The river water was useful for dying thread and the overall climate was conducive to spinning fine yarn. Ahmedabad was also situated in the heart of the cotton-growing areas in Gujarat and this ensured easy availability of raw material, while skilled and semi-skilled labour came in from across the state as well as from the adjoining state of Maharashtra. In 1965, the sixty-two textile mills in Ahmedabad employed about 1,30,000 people, one-tenth of the population of the city at that time.

A mill in the town of Kadi, in the adjoining district of Mehsana, was closing down. The prevalent thinking in the government was that the mill should be capitalised by constituting a State Textile Corporation to prevent loss of employment. This was after all the 1960s, the age of socialist thought, and nationalisation was very much the dominant logic of the day. The Industries department received a proposal for the mill to be taken over by the government.

I opposed it. I was clear that it would set the wrong precedent and create the economic and financial problems of moral hazard for the State. I could see that this was not about preventing one mill from shutting down. The headwinds for the entire textile industry were all too evident. There would be other mills that would also be closing down not too far in the future, and similar proposals for government takeover would come up. The government is not particularly known for its management efficiency and so over a period of time, this would result in a burgeoning financial burden on the government. Ultimately all the mills would have to be closed down but in the process, the government would have lost a lot of money and this would be a great drain on the government exchequer. I still remember the last sentence in my written note – 'Nationalisation is not the panacea for the ills afflicting the industry.'

My view was endorsed by the Secretary of the department as well. For a reason that fails memory, I was representing the department at the cabinet meeting instead of the Secretary. When the matter came up for discussion, the then Chief Minister said, "Samajpati, Bengalis, right from Raja Ram Mohan Ray to Subhash Chandra Bose, are known for their leftist ideology. But you seem to have a capitalist leaning." I stated that this was not a question of where I hailed from but rather a question of economic consideration, and that is what should prevail. Despite a strong case to the contrary, the government took a decision to set up the Gujarat State Textile Corporation and the mill was taken over.

Over the years, what I predicted came true to the letter. Taking over one fallen textile mill after another and saddled with years of financial losses, the Government had to ultimately wind up Gujarat State Textile Corporation. And when the corporation was being abolished after a couple of decades, the department happened to dig out the file which had my notings. They called me to say how prophetic the note had been. Unfortunately, a lot of public money had been wasted. And what was worse was that this story played out not just in the State but also at the Centre, where the National Textile Corporation was set up.

CHAPTER II

A Flying Projectile

Deputy Secretary, Industries, Ahmedabad

Tallow is essentially animal fat rendered for soapmaking and other end uses. While it has been a controversial ingredient and even had a role to play in the Sepoy Mutiny of 1857 when the grease used on cartridges for the Enfield rifle was rumoured to have tallow, it acts similar to palm oil, adding lather, stability and hardness to soap. Mutton tallow used to be a scarce commodity and was largely imported by the government. It was then distributed, with the Industries Commissioner allocating quantities to firms after due verification, and was never sold in the open market.

We received a complaint that a certain firm in Bhavnagar was procuring tallow from the government based on fraudulent documents, and instead of using it for manufacturing activity, was just selling it in the black market for easy money. An enquiry was commissioned and the report, confirming the allegations to be true, recommended that the firm should be blacklisted and necessary steps taken against the directors. We took prompt action as per the report, banning the company and ordering for the prosecution of the director, who, we soon understood, had strong connections with senior political functionaries.

One day, The Deputy Minister, Industries called me for a discussion on the 'mutton tallow' case. I went across to meet him with the file and shared the findings of the report as well as the facts that had come to light. He gave me a patient hearing but at the end of it, he said that the prosecution needed to be withdrawn. I was rather taken aback and told him that the evidence was overwhelming and given the facts, this was a clear case of intentional fraud and profiteering. Prosecuting the director was indeed the appropriate course of action and there were absolutely no grounds for its withdrawal.

It became apparent that other factors were at play and the Deputy Minister soon got very angry at my 'stubbornness', insisting that what he had said must be done. When he saw that he was not getting his way, he told me, "Samajpati, I am the Minister and you are a civil servant. You must obey my orders."

That was the tipping point for me. I was all of twenty-six years old and no one who knew me would say that I had a very measured temperament. I got up and flung the file in my hand towards him, perhaps with some force, asking him to communicate his order in writing. While it was not intended, the file flew through the air and hit the Deputy Minister with some velocity on the cheek. I walked out of the room.

Utsavbhai Parikh was the then Minister for Industries and the No. 2 in the cabinet after the Chief Minister. A prominent and powerful figure in the political sphere, he was a person of high integrity and ethical standards. As an aside, Utsavbhai later quit politics and renounced worldly ties to spend his last years at the Aurobindo Ashram in Pondicherry. I experienced an instance of his uprightness when I was in the Health Department, almost fifteen years later. I inadvertently came to know that his daughter and only child was a health worker in the department. She was facing some problem and had come to meet me with a brief note from her father. It read, "Samajpati, the bearer of this letter is my daughter. She is facing an issue at work. Please do the needful if the law permits, else kindly ignore the request she might have."

Back to the 'mutton tallow' case. After about a month of my heated exchange with the Deputy Minister, Utsavbhai called me over to discuss that file along with a few other items on the agenda. He enquired what had happened in my prior meeting with the Deputy Minister. On my narrating the sequence of events, he was aghast that his Deputy Minister had tried to intimidate an officer into doing an illegal act. In my presence, he buzzed for his stenographer and dictated a note to the Chief Minister stating, "I have gone through the matter. The Deputy Minister, Industries tried to browbeat the Deputy Secretary to carry out an illegal order which was rightly refused. Either he or I should head the Industries department." The Deputy Minister was subsequently dropped from the ministries without even an explanation being called for.

CHAPTER III

Guinea worms and Class rooms

District Development Officer, Banaskantha district, Palanpur

Arati and I got married in 1967. That was also the year I moved as DDO to Banaskantha – a district named after the West Banas River which runs through the valley between Mount Abu and the Aravalli Range, flowing into the plains of Gujarat and towards the Rann of Kutch. Quite unlike most of Gujarat, Banaskantha had almost ninety per cent of its population living in villages.

One of the first things I always did when I was posted to a new district, was to take a tour of the entire area. I would visit its towns and villages, meet the people and talk to them about the problems they were facing, their needs and their expectations. After all, it was them that I had a mandate to serve. This 'familiarisation visit' gave me a sweeping overview of the district and a great starting point for identifying my priorities and challenges. My Banaskantha induction took me to Vav, the largest taluka of the district.

I was struck by the fact that so many people appeared unwell and sick, and I found that they all seemed to be trying to remove some worms painstakingly from their legs one by one. This, I came to know, was the guinea worm disease. On probing a little further, I understood that the underlying reason was the kind of drinking water that the people were being supplied with. A person became infected when he or she drank water that contained guinea worm larvae. After some time the female worm would try to come out of the human body to lay her eggs resulting in a painful blister in the skin usually on a lower limb. At this time, it might become difficult to walk even a few steps. The only way to get rid of the disease even today is to try to roll the female worms out one by one as they break through the skin. There is no vaccination and no medication for this malady.

Apparently, the guinea worm issue was prevalent across the Santalpur and Vav areas. I was taken aback at the fact that even after twenty years of Independence we had not solved for such a basic requirement as safe drinking water. I took it upon myself to eradicate this problem across the length and breadth of the district. The other thing that stood out for me was that the abysmal education infrastructure – even primary schools were very few and far between. I had found my second mission.

Banaskantha was a large district, the second largest in the state, with 1300 villages spread over an area of 12703 sq. km. The water supply project that I had envisioned, therefore, was quite large and would have a significant cost impact beyond what was available in the budget. I relentlessly pursued the case for sanctioning of the required funds, with the government. Finally, the proposal for piped water supply to all villages in the district was approved. I was glad that the efforts had borne fruit. By the time I left Banaskantha the following year, I had kicked off the drinking water supply scheme for the district.

In terms of driving education, my goal was to provide for a primary school in every composite village. But the funds available proved woefully short for that kind of scale, and I was certain that the government would not allow for a quantum jump in the allocation for one district. In order to maximise the number of schools that we could build, I decided to raise part of the funds from the villages locally. I began going from village to village, talking to the panchayats, talking to rich farmers, talking to local business people, about the need for better education for their children. I would go with clear workings of what it would cost to build a school and run it, how much the government would put in and how much remained to be raised. The days were long and the travel grinding. I was totally absorbed by my work and my diet became very erratic. Lunch was rarely on time and many a time I would skip meals altogether. There was no bottled water those days, and often what I carried from home would be over well before I was back at night. This went on for weeks and months and ultimately took a toll on my health. I developed a stone in my kidney from the extensive travel. The doctors advised surgery. But I had no time to pause and rest. There was so much to be done. And it all seemed worth it when one could see new schools coming up in village after village, helping create a better future for the children.

In subsequent months, the problem with my kidneys worsened and I twice needed to be hospitalised at the speciality facility in Baroda. It was quite overwhelming to see people from Banaskantha fill trucks and come to Baroda to donate blood, upon hearing of my hospitalisation. Meanwhile, my 'dada' i.e. elder brother, who was based in Calcutta, came to know of my deteriorating health. He insisted that I leave the service immediately. Between life and the job, the choice, he said, was clear. I could put off my surgery no longer.

The operation took place in Calcutta. The surgery itself was done expertly but due to the negligence of one of the assisting doctors when the final stitches were sutured, I started bleeding uncontrollably post operation. The doctors gave me a five percent chance of survival as I went in for an emergency corrective surgery. Fortunately, I lived to tell this tale. The recovery was slow and it took me about five months to join my next posting at Jamnagar.

Many years later when I had moved to the Secretariat in the state capital of Gandhinagar, one day I received a post which curiously carried a Banaskantha sender address. I opened it. It was a book titled 'Banaskantha – On the Road to Progress' and I was surprised to find myself featured on the first page. Perhaps I did make a small difference during my stint in the district.

CHAPTER IV

Being the Shield

District Development Officer, Baroda district, Baroda

Baroda, Gujarat was my first posting in the civil services and I had just been promoted as the DDO (District Development Officer). The year was 1965 and the rains had been very scanty the previous monsoon. Major parts of the district were facing a drought and were declared 'scarcity affected'. It was my first encounter with a natural disaster.

At such times, the norm was to adopt a Keynesian approach and undertake additional public works – some of which were useful and some of which were taken up merely for employing local labourers and paying them some wages. Their work was physically taxing and once a week they were given a rest day, for which they were also to be paid an allowance. Since the district had not faced a drought in the recent past, no one seemed to know what the rest day allowance should be and the Executive Engineer brought the matter up to me. I referred this to my senior, the Collector of the district, but he too did not give a specific number. Instead, he invited my attention to certain pages of the Bombay Scarcity Manual. I found a formula which referred to the quantity of essential items like 'atta', oil, etc. that the allowance should be able to satisfy. The Executive Engineer calculated the amount as 75 paise and I gave a go-ahead.

A few days later, a flying squad from the State Revenue Department arrived. This was not abnormal because it was their job to keep a check on expenses being incurred in the scarcity hit districts. They completed their audit and pointed out that according to the standing orders of the Gujarat government, rest day allowance was to be paid at the rate of 50 paise per day and not 75 paise as had been done. It was news to me that there was a standing order available. Had we known this, we would not have had to make our own calculations. Anyway, we were now better informed and continued with our efforts trying to preserve both lives and livelihood through the tough times.

After a few weeks, I was in the office and my Executive Engineer came into my room in a state of panic. He said that the flying squad had escalated the audit issue and we had received a notice from the government. I asked him to calm down, take a seat and show me the communication. The notice called out the discrepancy in the rest day allowance rate amounting to an excess payment of Rs. 10 lacs. In addition, it stated that since the Executive Engineer was the signatory, this payment was to be recovered from him.

Now, the Executive Engineer was an elderly person on the verge of retirement. He was petrified at the prospect of having to cough up this huge sum and worried that his pension would be held up. Moreover, all he had from me was a verbal approval on the 75 paise rate and no written word that might come to his rescue.

I assured him he had nothing to worry. My reply to the notice stated that my Engineer had acted under my instructions. It was my decision and if any recovery was to be made, it should be made from the DDO and not from the Executive Engineer. The file for this case went through multiple levels, and after receiving the signature of the Revenue Secretary, reached the then Chief Secretary, Mr V.L. Gidwani. His response was short and crisp. He said it would have been highly appreciated if the Secretary,

Revenue Department, had examined this case more carefully and diligently. Gujarat government could easily survive without this pittance but the effect on the morale of the young officer who had just begun his career and had the courage to own up to his decision would be immense. The demand amount against the DDO was to be waived off unequivocally and immediately. He called me up to say that I had done the right thing and set the right example as a leader. This came as a big relief for my engineer and encouraged me to take bolder steps in the times to come.

CHAPTER V

Khooni

Collector, Panchmahals district, Godhra

Godhra, now known to many, for the start of one of the worst riots in recent Indian history, has always had a communally chequered past. Right after independence, in 1948, communal tensions led to an attempt on the life of Mr Pimputkar, the then-District Collector, though his bodyguard saved him while laying down his own life. Even in 1971, when I was moving in as Collector Panchmahals, of which Godhra was the headquarters, the district was prone to frequent communal flare-ups. Moreover, the overall law and order situation was rather poor, with several issues including women's safety.

There is an interesting bit of history around how Morarji Desai's journey to the position of Prime Minister of India began with a Godhra riot. In May 1930, he resigned as Deputy Collector of Godhra after being found guilty of going soft on Hindus during the riots of 1927-28. Morarji Desai wrote about this incident in his autobiography, The Story of my Life, in a chapter titled 'End of government service'. He wrote, "I had received a notice from the commissioner saying that the collector of Panchmahals had asked for an inquiry into my part in the riots. The burden of the issue framed by the commissioner was that I was a communalist and that I supported the Hindus against the Muslims. I received the government's decision in April 1930. No reasons were given for this conclusion. I was degraded by four places in the list of seniority." Morarji added, "After getting the arbitrary and unjust decision of the government, I made up my mind to resign from the service. I was worried only about what I should do after I resigned." Morarji did figure out what he wanted to do. He joined the national freedom movement under Mahatma Gandhi and later went on to become the first non-Congress Prime Minister of India in 1977.

Back to 1971. After I became District Collector, I was clear that I needed to control the law and order situation with a fair but firm hand and rein in the criminals. There was a notorious anti-social element who went by the trade name 'Khooni' or murderer and had several serious cases against him. He would kill people as if he were bringing down birds. But no one would ever stand up as a witness. That was the level of fear he commanded. After a few months of being in the job, my reputation as a tough and decisive official was fairly well known. I summoned Khooni to my chamber. He seemed a bit unnerved with the invitation but tried to maintain an air of nonchalance as he came in. He argued that people had unnecessarily given him a bad name and that he had no real criminal record. I told him that I had gone through his history sheet and was not interested in his defence. My communication to him was something along these lines, "Do listen carefully to what I am telling you. I don't know how long I will be here but if you play any mischief during my tenure, you will be dealt with firmly. On the other hand, if you behave according to the law, no harm will come to you." I think I must have communicated quite effectively. Khooni ran away from the district and never returned while I was there.

During my four years at Godhra, not a single riot took place (unfortunately sometime after my departure, the city descended into a year-long curfew). I would tell the Hindu leaders to ensure that they obeyed the law at all times and take no liberties for being in the majority. I would equally tell the Muslim leaders, if there is an attack on your community, I will protect you. But if you create any trouble, there will be no laxity. Despite my being a Hindu by religion, I think I was quite popular with the Muslim leaders because they knew that I would not tolerate any provocation from either side. One of my acquaintances at Godhra, Mr Ahmed, continued to stay in touch and became a close family friend over the years. Decades later, after I had retired from the civil services, he even offered a personal loan when I had to pay for my son's MBA at IIM Calcutta and my bank balance was proving quite inadequate for the fees.

CHAPTER VI

On the Donkey's Back

Collector, Panchmahals district, Godhra

When I went to Godhra as Collector Panchmahals, Chimanbhai Patel was the Industries Minister. In July 1973, he became the Chief Minister replacing Ghanshyam Oza. Little did he know that he would soon face a mass movement which would result in his ouster in less than a year.

A few months after Chimanbhai's taking over, there were allegations of corruption, specifically that he had granted favours to the oil-lobby of Rajkot allowing for inflation in groundnut oil prices. There was a cascading effect of the oil price hike on food prices. In December 1973, students of L.D. College of Engineering, Ahmedabad went on a strike to protest against a 20% hike in food prices at the hostel mess. A similar demonstration organised two weeks later at Gujarat University, resulted in clashes between police and students and that provoked students throughout the state. Soon, there was a call given for an indefinite strike across educational institutions in the state. Thus began the 'Nav-nirman Andolan'.

The initial demands were related to food and education. But it quickly escalated into a demand for the Chief Minister's resignation and the agitation began to turn violent. Middle-class people and some factory workers also joined the protests in Ahmedabad and ration shops were attacked. A state-wide strike was organised on the 25th of January which resulted in clashes between police and people in over 33 towns. The violence intensified and the army was called in to restore normalcy in cities like Ahmedabad.

Godhra, the headquarters of Panchmahals district, was not immune to the state-wide agitation and students were protesting here too. One day, they gave a call for a personal attack on Somalal Shiroia, the MLA from the city, who was seen to be close to the Chief Minister. They announced that the following day his head would be shaven, buttermilk would be poured on it and he would be made to sit on a donkey's back and paraded through the main bazaar. This was inspired by a similar aggression in another district a day before, which had received widespread coverage in media.

That afternoon, Somalal came to meet me visibly shaken by the threat. He made a request, "Please allow me to stay at your house tonight, otherwise, I will be humiliated and tortured tomorrow. They could even kill me." I told him he had nothing to fear, and that if he was harmed despite my knowing of the planned attack, I was not worthy of the post that I was holding. I said, "I am aware of the call given by the agitators and their threat to assault you at your house at 8 a.m. You do not need to find a place to hide. I will be there at your place at 7.30 a.m. Rest assured, you shall be at your house tomorrow morning and you shall be safe. That is my word to you."

It was clear to me that this situation needed to be dealt with a firm hand. The MLA faced imminent danger. Also, if I allowed the agitation in Godhra to take a violent turn, things could spiral out of control across the entire district causing irreparable damage to life and property. Fortunately, I had been at Panchmahals for almost two years by then and had acquired a fairly formidable reputation as a 'no-nonsense' officer. I could draw upon that. Also, I was not dealing with seasoned criminals. After all, these were just students albeit some with political motivations. They would have a definite fear of the law.

I called the agitating leaders to my office in the evening. I told them, "I am aware of the call you have given. But if you execute the plan, I would only request you to visualise the face of your grieving mother."

I am not sure if Somalal Shiroia slept well that night despite my assurances. At 7.30 the next morning, I was there at his residence in person and so was a well-equipped police contingent. I stayed till 11.30 a.m. No one had risked turning up.

CHAPTER VII

When the Heavens Opened up

Collector, Panchmahals district, Godhra

It was a pleasant Sunday morning in the month of September. My wife was away to Calcutta, appearing for her MA exams. I was sitting relaxed with my feet up on the table and reading a newspaper with no one to hurry me up for breakfast. The loud ring of the phone suddenly broke my state of 'nirvana'. It was the Mamlatdar of Sahara taluka and he informed that the taluka was flooded. I couldn't believe it and reconfirmed if I had heard it right. "Floods?" I asked again. The last one in Panchmahals had happened in 1920 more than fifty years ago! This was a district that was used to facing droughts, not floods. The Mamlatdar replied in the affirmative.

I went to the Control Room right away and did not return home for seven days as I took charge of the relief and rescue operations. There was not a moment to breathe as I was pressing emergency actions into motion across the affected districts and trying to organise a coordinated response – there were no cellphones then and even landlines would easily give in during such times. It was manic. The flood had caught us totally unawares with its abruptness, its intensity and its spread. I later came to know that Rajasthan had callously released vast amounts of water from its upstream dams on the river Banas without any intimation to Gujarat government. The already raised water levels due to the monsoon rains, quickly breached danger levels leading to the floods.

I used to have a Deputy Collector called Purohit, an elderly gentleman handling scarcity operations, who had put in his papers for a more relaxed pace to life and gone back to his home town of Chhota Udaipur. He had worked with me earlier too as a TDO (Taluka Development Officer) in Baroda district. When he saw the news of the floods in the papers, he rushed to Godhra and came to meet me straight away. He wanted to resume work and be there to support me in this hour of crisis. I told him that there was going to be intense pressure over the next few weeks and that he should not put himself through it, especially at his age. But he insisted that this was an emergency and he absolutely must be there. I gave in. Purohit joined me in the Control Room and worked side by side. We were monitoring the flood situation in the affected districts by the hour and galvanising the fire-brigade, the police and other government departments into rescue and relief operations. Thousands of people were being moved, boats were evacuating people from terraces, low-flying helicopters were undertaking tricky manoeuvers to pick up people who had climbed onto trees, food packets were being airdropped, and relief shelters were being set up. In the Control Room, we were working round the clock under extraordinary pressure. I said, "Purohit, I am much younger. You should at least have some food because of your diabetes and grab a bit of rest." But he did not pay any heed and kept at it without a break. On Day 3 of the operations, he suddenly collapsed - right in front of my eyes. With little food, water and rest his body could take the physical and mental strain no more and he passed away. It was an exemplary act of selfless service. I wept uncontrollably that day. But I had to carry on.

Meanwhile, the floods were unrelenting. We needed to move hundreds of people from low lying areas around Godhra, which were submerged, to higher ground at the headquarters. Arrangements had been made for providing temporary shelter and food. But many of these areas were now unreachable by road and evacuating people was becoming increasingly difficult. We were running out of time and options as the water levels were rising rapidly.

I came to know that a train from Delhi was scheduled to pass through the city. I made a quick decision and ordered all passengers to be de-boarded at Godhra station. We would divert the train to rescue the stranded people. Once that was done, the passengers would continue their onward journey after a forced break of about six hours. At that time, the MP from Godhra, an influential politician was on that train too and refused to get off. But we were losing time and ultimately the police had to forcibly de-board him. The train was diverted to bring in the flood-affected people and it then resumed its onward journey.

Subsequently, the MP complained against me in a letter to the Prime Minister, Indira Gandhi, saying that there was an unlawful diversion of the train and that he was manhandled at Godhra railway station. Since this was done under my instructions, strict action should be taken against me. I knew nothing about the complaint. The Prime Minister sent the letter to the then Chief Minister, Chimanbhai Patel for inquiry and report. Chimanbhai called me up. By then the floods had started receding and the situation was nearing normalcy so I was able to leave the headquarters and meet him in the state capital. He briefed me about the letter to the Prime Minister and asked me what had happened. I described the circumstances under which I took the extraordinary decision to divert the train. He was supportive and congratulated me on having done the right thing, and asked me not to worry. Chimanbhai went to Delhi, met Indira Gandhi and explained to her the context for the action. She too saw that the step was taken keeping public interest paramount and was appreciative of it. The MP's complaint was shelved.

CHAPTER VIII

Shoot at Sight

Collector, Panchmahals district, Godhra

The Godhra Collector's bungalow, a hangover from our colonial past, was impressive in its architecture and expansive in its layout. With eight rooms and huge balconies, a delightful marble water fountain, sprawling gardens with sandalwood trees and brilliant blossoms manned by a skilled team of gardeners, one could almost mistake it for a small palace. I was standing on the verandah on a leisurely Sunday morning, trying to get in an eyeful of the beautiful view of the gardens with its colourful flowers in full bloom.

My peon Mansukh, called out,"Saheb, there's a phone call." Mrs Pathak, wife of the District Congress President was on the line. I could hear the panic in her voice. She said, "Sir, my house has been surrounded by Nav-nirman agitators. There are tens of them and they are planning to burn down our house. We have no way to escape. They will kill my husband and me."

The Nav-nirman agitation was at its peak in the state. What had started off as a peaceful protest, had quickly escalated into a violent agitation. There were widespread strikes, arson and looting, all targeting the state government. Protesters had begun attacking the vehicles and property of the legislators and corporators of the ruling party to intimidate them into resigning. Even apolitical government functionaries were being targeted and there had been recent assaults on District Collectors too. We had successfully prevented the protests from turning violent in

Panchmahals thus far, but the phone call rang in a change of stance by the agitating student leaders.

I was in my pyjamas and vest. There was not a moment to lose. I just put on a t-shirt over my vest and left for the Pathak residence. The seconds seemed like minutes as I stepped on the gas and drove full throttle. The DSP (District Superintendent of Police) had been informed too and as I approached the house, I could see him turning into the lane with support personnel in tow, almost simultaneously. I could also see scores of protestors with lots of kerosene cans all around the house and a totally surcharged atmosphere.

I had to make a quick decision. I asked the DSP to announce on the loudspeaker that the crowd had five minutes within which they must start dispersing otherwise a 'shoot at sight' order would be executed. I climbed onto the top of the jeep as the message blared out from the loudspeaker. The student leaders needed to know that the District Collector was present right there to follow up on the threat. My assessment was that given my reputation and the strong police presence, the announcement would be taken seriously allowing us to de-escalate the situation without any firing. In case this did not materialise, my Plan B was to fire downwards towards the legs of the violent protestors. Shooting in the air was not even an option that crossed my mind. With a highly incensed mob like this, if you fire in the air you will always end up with a higher loss of life in the process. Various studies on riot situations have established this almost as a fact. Blank firing would only serve to get the crowd more excited. They would start thinking that they are not going to be fired at, and become emboldened to take a more aggressive stance. Ultimately you would have to open greater defensive fire on an increasingly agitated and menacing mob leading to a larger loss of life. Thankfully, Plan A worked.

As soon as the announcement was made, the agitators panicked and started running helter-skelter. In about ten minutes the crowd had dispersed entirely and not a single bullet was fired. The protesters had left in such a flurry that the place was strewn with leftover slippers, shoes, wallets and even shirts. The DSP and Iwent in to meet the Pathaks who were heaving a sigh of relief and thanked us profusely. We were happy with the outcome too.

CHAPTER IX

Biting the Bullet

Deputy Secretary, Health Department, Ahmedabad

For India, our population is more of a problem than a dividend. The government recognised this soon after Independence and in 1951, India became the first country in the developing world to create a state-sponsored family planning program. The program's primary objective was to lower fertility rates and slow population growth in order to accelerate economic development. This remained the dominant thinking of successive governments even though there might have been the odd deviation in the discourse. For instance, during the United Nations Population Conference in Bucharest in 1974, India's Minister for Family Planning, Karan Singh, famously said, "Development is the best contraceptive." That is indeed true but in a poor country like India, with ever-increasing hands reaching out for limited resources, it is difficult to kick start the development cycle in the first instance.

Family planning continued to be the No. 1 priority for the Health Department when I joined in the late 1970s. While mass sterilisation was the established route to family planning, there were several methods being used across the developing world. I wanted to understand these better to be able to decide on the right approach for our context.

Indonesia had achieved very good results in this area despite it being a country where one might expect significant religious objection to the idea of family planning. I visited Indonesia and stayed in their villages for a month to understand their system. One learning was that while contraception is the couple's responsibility, most men don't see it that way. It is women who usually take primary responsibility for birth control, as they have to handle pregnancy and child care. The Indonesian approach was based on the use of contraceptive pills. Besides awareness programs, they had interesting habit-building interventions such as the ringing of the village bell at 8 p.m. every day to serve as a reminder for 'pill-time'. They also had inspectors undertaking audits at a household level, to check whether the pills were being taken as scheduled.

But the typical Indonesian village was a little island, much smaller and more compact than its Indian counterpart. Women were also more aware and educated on the average, and had fewer taboos around the topic. I was surprised to find that they did not hesitate to talk about family planning even with someone like me, a total stranger from another country. So, there were significant differences between the two countries, and I felt that the birth-control pill would meet with too many execution challenges back in India. Besides, the alternate route, surgery, would be more effective and permanent as a solution. The challenge however, was to find a way where this could be undertaken at the scale that India needed.

After evaluating available options along with medical experts, I initiated the use of laparoscopic operation in a camp environment, a first for India. Laparoscopic sterilisation had several advantages – it was quick, effective and less cumbersome for women, most of whom could go home 2–4 hours after the procedure. But until then, it was done only in a hospital environment and therefore accessible to very few. The hesitation to take it wider into health camps was also accentuated by a UN report which pointed at the need for well-equipped centres and good infrastructure. But I saw that this method could be India's answer given the right pre-operative preparation, surgical skill, and post-operative care. It seemed worth biting the bullet.

Back then the equipment was not available in India. We imported it from Germany and launched the first few camps. The operating surgeons were trained by expert doctors from Ahmedabad. While the early sterilisation camps were very successful, there were, unfortunately, two or three surgeries which resulted in complications. This was exactly the moment the naysayers were waiting for, prominent among whom was the advisor to the Health Ministry in Delhi. He sent a scathing report against the approach and against me, in particular, stating that I was not a technical person but insisted on ignoring expert advice. Sarla Grewal, who subsequently became the principal secretary to Rajiv Gandhi, was the Family Planning Commissioner at the Centre. She called me over to Delhi but met me with an open mind. After understanding the merits of the case she gave me a clean chit saying that this initiative should be encouraged and not discouraged. She called in the advisor and said that she had no need for his services any longer.

We scaled up the laparoscopy sterilisation camps across the state and they proved to be highly acceptable, economical, speedy, and safe. The method was adopted throughout India and became the primary route to Family Planning for the country.

Gujarat ranked first in the country in Family Planning for all the four years that I was in charge. When I was leaving, I still remember Sarla Grewal's comment, "The Health department of Gujarat has been orphaned."

CHAPTER X

Blink First, Never

Secretary, Panchayats and Rural Housing, Gandhinagar
During my tenure as Secretary, I was faced with a state-wide panchayat employees strike. There was a pay differential between State Government employees and Panchayat employees and salary equalisation was one of several demands. The union struck a strident cord in the discussions with the government and achieved a near-universal implementation. Critical government activities were being managed by the DDOs directly with little support at the ground level. With an indefinite strike, the aim was to hold the government to ransom and get the demands approved.

The then Chief Secretary of Gujarat was perhaps not the best person in a crisis, and a state-wide indefinite strike easily breached his anxiety threshold. He was petrified that the panchayat machinery had come to a halt and started calling me up almost every hour for updates. I tried to assure him that I was on it and requested him to allow for the negotiations to play out over the following few days. Yet he would call me for meetings incessantly and seek telephonic updates round the clock. I was finding it difficult to focus on solving the problem at hand and was totally frustrated.

I met the Chief Minister, Madhavsinh Solanki and told him that I would appreciate it if I could be moved out of the Panchayat department. He had known me for many years and his surprise at my apparent retreat in the face of this strike was easy to sense. I told him that I would never shy away from a challenge, but it was becoming impossible to operate given the constant interference by the Chief Secretary. There wasn't much being suggested by way of direction but there was one question being repeated over and over again, "What's the update Samajpati?" I was struggling to think clearly and take the necessary steps. Madhavsinh assured me that I would get a free hand. He spoke to the Chief Secretary, asking him to allow greater operating freedom to the Secretaries. He added, "If they fail, haul them up but don't impinge on their decision making." He made a specific reference to the interactions with me as an example and asked him to focus more on the overall administration of the state.

The calls stopped. I felt free to deal with the problem at hand and rolled up my sleeves. I wanted to teach the union leaders a lesson for trying to push the government to the wall and force it to meet their demands, instead of discussing across the table. What irked me further was that in one of the meetings, a union leader had abused the then Health Secretary who happened to be a lady. The Essential Services Maintenance Act was invoked and the key leaders of the strike were arrested. In the next few meetings with the union, I took a very aggressive and uncompromising stance. I told them unambiguously, that not a single point would be conceded by the government and that they could continue the strike for as long as they wanted to. They would have to unconditionally withdraw the strike and tender an apology to the Health Secretary. Nothing less. I issued a clear warning, "The government will dismiss all of you and announce fresh recruitments. We will fight it out in the Supreme Court if need be, hiring a top pleader. You can go and fight your case there." This unyielding approach was always my preferred method for handling strikes. For, if one started to make concessions, there would be no end to it. The message I always sought to establish upfront was that this strike will be futile and yield nothing.

The strike had gone on for twenty days. Now the union leaders were in a quandary. The Chief Minister was not giving them an appointment. If they contacted the Chief Secretary, they were being redirected to me with whom they were able to make no headway. Meanwhile, the leaders were getting arrested and as per the rules if they stayed behind bars for more than twenty-four hours, they were automatically suspended and their salaries withheld. They were left with no option.

One day, the union leaders came to meet me and said that they were withdrawing the agitation along with an apology to the lady Health Secretary. I spoke to her to confirm if she was satisfied with their expression of regret. Once she replied in the affirmative, I wrote to inform the Chief Minister that the Panchayat Union strike had been unconditionally called off. Madhavsinh replied, "Thanks, very much".

Some years later, I had moved to another department and was getting off at a bus stand in Gandhinagar. There was an ongoing joint strike by state and panchayat employees and those very union leaders happened to be present at the bus stand. On seeing me, they came across to exchange greetings and I asked them how things were. They smilingly said, "Sir, it's good that you are no longer in the department. We are very happy. We have already got fifty percent of our demands through and in today's meeting we will have another ten to fifteen points cleared. Had you been around, we would have had to return empty handed."

CHAPTER XI

A Clean Sweep

Secretary, Forests and Environment, Gandhinagar

My initial days in the Forest Department were an eye-opener and I found the extent of corruption difficult to fathom. I had never seen anything like this before. At the end of my first three months, I placed twenty-one officers and staff under suspension, at one stroke, on differing corruption charges.

As I was getting inducted into the department, it was plain to see the many loopholes and opportunities for malpractice. But finding solutions would need me to get to the bottom of the money-making mechanism. The starting point was to identify the sources of leakage, of which there were many. I could distil it down to two prime culprits.

One was 'cutting of trees'. The Forest Department used to officially permit felling of a limited number of trees every year. A teak tree, for instance, reaches full maturity in forty to fifty years. Sometimes, it would then need to be cut to make way for new trees to grow. Now let's say there is an official approval for the felling of five hundred trees. Unofficially, the local functionaries would be hand in glove with the contractor and allow, say, five thousand trees to be cut. As I write this article in 2020, a teak tree sells at about a lac and a half rupees. So the kind of money to be made from the excess felling was enormous and everyone right from politicians to senior forest officials to the beat guard would then get their share of the booty.

The second source was 'sapling plantation'. The first week of July is typically observed as 'Van Mahotsav', an annual tree-planting festival started in 1950 by K.M. Munshi, the then Union Minister for Agriculture and Food. The main objective behind starting this celebration was to create awareness amongst people about planting trees and conserving our forests. Little could he have imagined the creative use that the festival would be put to, down the years. One District Forest Officer (DFO) would say, for instance, that he has raised 2 crore saplings at the cost of Rs. 7 per sapling. He would submit a bill for Rs. 14 cr. Now, who could go and count two crore of these saplings? Then he would plant the saplings and raise a second bill for another Rs. 14 cr, neatly breaking the 'cost' into heads such as the cost of digging a hole of 2x3 sq.ft., watering cost and labour cost. When I would go for a visit and find no saplings where they were supposed to be, I would be told, "Sir, they have all dried up. We tried a lot but the weather has been so hot and there have been no rains at all." I was dumbfounded, how does one even trace anything in a situation like this! I introduced a logbook where specific measurements of the hole were to be maintained so that at least these could be cross-verified. But the problem persisted. They would enter details in the logbook but on being questioned would have convenient reasons, "It rained so heavily the seedling has been destroyed and we can't even see the hole."

The extent and pervasiveness of malpractice was just mind-boggling. It was time for some corrective measures. I issued an order that banned the cutting of trees in any forest area in Gujarat, altogether for a period of five years. If trees were found cut in any zone, the responsible person would be placed under suspension, pending enquiry and final punishment.

For the planting of saplings, the system earlier was that a bill would be raised directly. I put in place a process where a plan would need to be submitted first with details of which stretch of land was going to be used, how many saplings were to be planted, etc. Only upon approval could any work be initiated. Checks and balances were also introduced for prompt verification of the job upon completion.

These were the policy and process measures. But corruption was so endemic in the department that I was certain I had to take some visible measures and send a strong signal that it would not be tolerated any longer. I undertook an exercise to verify previous corruption complaints which were lying unattended and also had surprise visits conducted to identify cases of malpractice. I remember myself going into forests in the middle of the night to catch illegal felling. Based on the audit, we could identify twenty-one employees of the department whose actions seemed strongly mala fide. They were placed under suspension. Now, 'suspension' of a government servant is a very significant action with far-reaching effect. People under suspension cannot discharge their duties and must remain at home, drawing only fifty per cent of their salary. If found not guilty after an inquiry, they are reinstated. And if guilt is proven, depending on the gravity, appropriate action is taken such as dismissal, withholding of increment or pension, delaying of promotion and others.

The announcement of suspension created havoc in the entire department and sent a shiver down the spine of the corrupt. Along with the other measures on the policy and process front, it successfully put a stop to the huge leakages that were taking place across the organisation. There were vested interests both within and in the political class who even tried to manoeuvre my transfer and approached the minister. But I had just come in, it was too early to justify a transfer.

CHAPTER XII

Not a Postman

Secretary, Forests and Environment, Gandhinagar

The Forest Department, as also the Home Department, are a bit different structurally from most others in as much as that the officers belong to another service (in this case the Indian Forest Service) whereas the department head is from the IAS. This oftentimes creates some friction between the Secretary and the top department officials and results in the existence of two power centres.

There was a scheduled round of transfers due in the department. The proposal for general transfer of officers across levels came in from the Principal Conservator of Forest (PCF). For me, getting the right officer in the right position was perhaps one of the most critical decisions in order to enhance overall department performance. In all organisations, there is some deadwood - people from whom it is very difficult to inspire performance. At times in the government, one finds a relatively lower focus on outcomes. This, coupled with a general aversion to dismissing non-performers, often results in a fairly high deadwood percentage. One of my ways of solving for this problem was to ensure that in key positions, there were some stars who would punch above their weight and drive things forward. I spent time and effort in identifying these good performers and giving them the right opportunities. A key performance input for me was the Monthly Review Meeting. I used to conduct almost a hundred point review each month with key officers across the state. After the review, I would write a demi-official letter summarizing the action points and timelines agreed in the meeting, and review these again in the following meeting. Besides, I used to tour extensively and work with the officers in the field to assess their performance. In short, when it came to people, I got into a fair bit of detail and as a result, had a strong point of view.

So when the proposal came in, I took a thorough look at the recommended transfers and made a fair number of changes to ensure key roles were well-manned and, in some cases, individual biases removed. The PCF wanted to have things his way but he knew I would make necessary modifications to the plan. So he tried to influence the outcome through an alternate route.

All transfer proposals in the government go through the General Administration Department (GAD). So GAD does wield significant influence on people movements and, where there is power, there are power brokers. At that time, there was a Section Officer, a position fairly low down in the hierarchy, who used to be quite influential. When the transfer file went to the GAD, he wrote that the Secretary, Forests and Environment had made a lot of changes despite the fact that he would not know the officers involved. So, he recommended that the original proposal of the PCF be approved instead. That note was then endorsed by the Chief Secretary and after all due signatures, the file came back to me.

I was quite shocked to see that my recommendations, as Head of the Department, were not approved. To me, it was an affront to my capability, a discounting of my contribution and a blatant disregard of my role. I wrote to the chief secretary, "I do not wish to work as a postman. If I have to do my job, I must work as an effective secretary of the department. If the government feels that I am incapable of leading the Forests and Environment department, it is free to move me to a job it sees more appropriate. Secondly, according to convention, if the Secretary of a department puts up a note, only the Secretary, Personnel should put up a dissenting note and not the Section Officer. In this case, that practice has also not been followed."

The Chief Secretary read my note and realised that I was not pleased with the sequence of events which led to my inputs as the Secretary being totally ignored. He also saw the procedural flaw in terms of the dissenting note. It was nice of him to write back apologising for not having gone through the file in full detail in the first instance. He also affirmed his full confidence in me and said, "Having reviewed the file, the proposal of the Secretary, Forests and Environment is approved in toto."

CHAPTER XIII

Taking on Big Business

Secretary, Forests and Environment, Gandhinagar

When I was at the Secretariat, there used to be a designated day of the week, Tuesday - if my memory serves me right, when Secretaries of all departments were supposed to be in the capital and people could come and meet them without prior appointment. On one such day, some villagers from Kheda district came to see me. They complained about the discharge of chemicals from a factory in Ahmedabad. Their village was downstream and because of the continuous dumping of effluents, the land had become infertile and it had become difficult to grow crops to earn their livelihood. They also showed the effect the polluted water had on their skin, and how the skin on their legs and hands had peeled off. I assured them that I would look into the matter and asked them why the issue had not been raised earlier. There was dejection and anger in their response. Apparently, countless attempts had been made over the years but all the pleas had fallen on deaf ears. The factory was owned by the brother of one of the most powerful businessmen in the country. I communicated a date on which I would visit the village.

On the conveyed date, I arrived at the village in Kheda. What the villagers had told me was indeed true. I saw for myself the widespread damage caused by effluents both on the fertility of the soil and on the health of the people. Since I would be passing by Ahmedabad on my way back, I thought I would go to the company's office, meet the promoter and persuade him to take corrective measures.

As an aside, my wife and I had attended his son's wedding reception and if my memory serves me right, it was not too long before this episode. I broke my return journey at Ahmedabad. When I explained the issue to the promoter, he seemed to be aware of it and did not dispute the facts. But he was rather rude when I requested his intervention. He remarked, "What you are saying makes no sense. If I now put up an effluent treatment plant, do you know how much it will cost – 10 crores! And what is the return I get? Do you think that just because you suggest something I have to do it without looking at its implication on my business?" One could sense the arrogance from having connections at high places and also a bit of disdain for this young bureaucrat who seemed rather green behind the ears. I realised there was no point in trying to explain further, and resumed my road trip back to the Secretariat in Gandhinagar.

Upon reaching, I asked the Pollution Control Board, which was under the Department, to serve a notice to the company that they were to put up a treatment plant at the factory within 3 months, failing which they would have to lock it down. I knew this meant taking on one of the most powerful businesspersons in the country head-on. It would be child's play for him to have me transferred out for creating trouble. He would not even have to meet anyone personally for this. A short phone call from one of his government 'handlers' would probably be enough.

But I was never one to give up without a fight, no matter how difficult the odds. The truth was on my side and that, for me, was always the biggest strength. And in this case, out of sheer happenstance, I had some other factors in my favour. TN Seshan was the Secretary, Forests and Environment at the Centre and also an advisor to the then

Prime Minister, Rajiv Gandhi. We shared a similar 'no-nonsense' approach to work and got along quite well. Sarla Grewal, who I had worked with closely when I was Deputy Secretary, Health was a big supporter and had famously said when I moved on from the department, "Today, the Health Department of Gujarat has been orphaned." So in a way, I had the ears of the Prime Minister.

I called up Seshan as soon as I had asked for the notice to be served to the company. After explaining the situation to him, I told him that I was taking on the business house, and sought his support. He said, "Don't worry. Go ahead. Do what is right. I am there." Seshan knew that he had to take preemptive action right away. A call went out from the PMO (Prime Minister's Office) that the Secretary, Forests and Environment, Gujarat could not be shifted without the prior permission of the PMO.

The notice for the treatment plant was issued. First, the company tried to use its relationships with the Chairman of the Pollution Control Board. While I do not have first-hand information, I am quite certain that the political leaders in the state would have been spoken to and they would have conveyed their inability to affect the matter because of the PMO. Ultimately, this episode ended in a meeting between one of the most powerful businessmen in the country and the Prime Minister. Rajiv Gandhi had been thoroughly briefed by Seshan about this issue. In the meeting, he maintained that all actions had been taken in accordance with the law, so nothing could be done.

I thanked Seshan for his support. The treatment plant was put up and the villagers got their rightful due. The business house was nice enough to invite me to the inauguration ceremony.

CHAPTER XIV

Molten Gold at Rs. 28

Managing Director, Grofed, Ahmedabad

After a tussle with my political bosses, I was banished to Grofed (Gujarat Cooperative Oilseed Growers' Federation), a post who's only claim to fame was perhaps its insignificance. I was to head a business which had all of Rs. 50 crore to report as its highest turnover since its inception. So it was almost a defunct organisation with hardly any activity. I knew this was a punishment posting but I thought maybe I could undertake some expansion and see what could be done. Someone had once remarked, "If Samajpati is posted as a police constable, he will treat that as the most important job and transform it into one too."

I studied the oilseeds market and found that there indeed was a lot of scope for expansion for the organisation across several untapped whitespaces. On the one hand, the domestic market presented a huge opportunity, or rather a pressing need to provide consumers with branded, good-quality products and, on the other hand, we could exploit the export market more aggressively for by-products.

The only branded play Grofed had then was a small brand called Kiran in groundnut oils. But the groundnut oils from Gujarat had a problem - the significant presence of alphatoxins which are a kind of contamination caused by moulds. This can occur both during the production season as well as during post-harvest handling and can lead to adverse health effects on humans and animals alike. So I decided against promoting groundnut oils and instead targeted the mustard oil segment which was large, especially in eastern India. Periodically, one would also come across newspaper reports of people falling ill by consuming mustard oil sold through the public distribution system and other retail outlets. Our aim was to replace these low-quality products with pure, unadulterated oil. Quality became my obsession and our purpose.

We developed a coherent strategy to execute on our purpose. There were five mills largely lying idle that were owned by us. We re-started them so that we could ourselves undertake the crushing of oilseeds and control production. During product development, someone from the team suggested that just like the current products in the market, we should add an ingredient which increases pungency, since consumers had a preference for the sharp taste in mustard oil. However, this ingredient also had some detrimental effects which manufacturers used to ignore. I summarily shot this proposal down. I would not put the health of my consumers at risk for enhancing taste, but instead, drive appeal by delivering great value. We innovated on the packaging. Thus far, if consumers wanted a branded product and not loose oil, they had to purchase it in unwieldy tin cans of five or ten litres. For the first time in the country, we introduced edible oil in PET bottles of one litre. These bottles were not available in India, so we imported them from West Germany. Our manufacturing and product strategy was ready.

Our marketing platform was 'purity' which tied in perfectly with our purpose of 'quality'. We launched the products under a new brand 'Arati' which had positive associations with prayer and purity. I must admit here, the fact that my wife is also called by the same name is not a complete coincidence. I was aware that as a new player, a compelling marketing campaign would be critical. We engaged with leading advertising agencies and narrowed down on Tara Sinha Associates as our communications partner.

The advertising idea of 'Molten Gold' was born over several rounds of discussions. Since mustard oil has a golden colour and gold is seen as pure and precious, there was an intrinsic connection with the product. And it drew in women instantly, who were after all the decision-makers in this case. The launch began with a teaser campaign in Calcutta, which simply said 'Molten Gold at Rs. 28'. One fine morning, the city woke up to see this message plastered all over. It piqued everyone's curiosity and had people guessing what it might all be about. A Bengali newspaper even suggested that it was a signal that gold prices would crash. We had people talking about it in buses and tea stalls. In an age when there was no Whatsapp and Facebook, this was a campaign that entered social conversation like nothing before. Sujit Sanyal, a leading adman of our times, who went on to create advertising for many multinational companies, in his book 'Life in a Rectangle' calls this 'one of the most exciting and successful campaigns of my career'.

After the teaser, I revealed the product, to extensive press and television coverage. The launch led to unprecedented trials. And when people tasted the oil, they vouched for its quality. In fact, we announced that if anyone could prove adulteration in the product they would get a handsome monetary reward. We backed our claims with action, setting up a public testing laboratory where anyone could walk in and test their oil, not just Arati but also other competing brands. I was obsessed about ensuring quality. No batch went through without testing and certification and I made frequent visits to the factory shop floor to check samples and also to send the right message across the organisation.

We swamped the market starting with West Bengal and then expanded all over eastern India to Bihar, Orissa and Assam. There was a very well established, hundred-year-old brand called 'Ganesh' which my father and grandfather also used to consume. The promoters came to meet me, offering royalty in lieu of a pause in sales of the Arati brand in the East. But there was no way I was going to stop. We had seen success and were already planning on the next segments to enter. I sensed that we could solve the problem of adulteration in the oil sector for the entire country. We also started rapidly expanding our export of oil cakes to the West.

In a single year, Grofed moved from a turnover of Rs. 50 crores to Rs. 500 crores! It was insignificant no longer. The spectacular success galvanised the entire organisation and the team found new meaning and purpose in their work.

SNAPSHOTS (Chapters XV-XXXVI)

Interesting incidents, sometimes funny, read at a brisk pace

CHAPTER XV

Vast Ocean Theory

Assistant Collector, Baroda

During our early postings in the district, one of my batchmates posted in the adjoining district of Bharuch, used to frequent Baroda. He used to say, "Don't try to swim against the current, swim with it. The ocean is vast. How long will you keep swimming against the flow? The smarter thing is to swim along with the tide." He was referring to my working long hours and going up against people with vested interests. My batch mate further explained, "Once you leave the post, the next person will come and all your effort will be of no avail. So don't try to go out of your way to change things." I termed this his 'Vast Ocean' theory.

But my perspective was a bit different. According to me, the greatest aspect of the service was that it gave one an opportunity to serve the country, especially the poor and less privileged. One should take that opportunity and serve to the best of one's ability. For me, it was not about the pomp and show. It was about doing your duty, about doing your job as best as you can.

CHAPTER XVI

Firing in Self-defence

Assistant Collector, Baroda

There were ongoing state-wide agitations against the rise in the price of groundnut oil. I was parked at the guest house in a sensitive taluka called Padra to control the situation on the ground. At around 8 a.m., I received a message that agitators were going to burn down the (Taluka Development Officer) TDO's office. The Assistant Collector had no vehicle at his disposal those days. So I left the guest house immediately and started walking towards the TDO's office with a police constable in tow. Just outside the guest house, we had to cross a large patch of marshy land and take extremely slow, laborious steps through it. The agitators spotted me and knew that if they attacked me there, it would be impossible for me to escape.

A mob of about thirty agitators surrounded us and started moving menacingly towards the constable and me. It was a life and death situation. I ordered the constable to fire in the air but he was trembling and paralysed with fear. I snatched the rifle from him and after firing in the air in self-defence, pointed the gun towards the approaching agitators. They were not armed and seeing my aggressive posture, beat a hasty retreat. By the time they regrouped, we were able to get out of the swamp and reach the TDO's office where additional police reinforcement was present. It was a close call.

CHAPTER XVII

War Story

Assistant Collector, Baroda

In September 1965, J.N. Chaudhuri, the Chief of Army Staff was on a routine visit to Srinagar. While he was on his way back, he got the news that Kashmir had been attacked. Thus began the 1965 war, a culmination of skirmishes that took place between April and September that year, between Pakistan and India. The Indian Army was not fully prepared and tried to open a new front in the Lahore sector but could not succeed in the attempt.

An emboldened Pakistan took a more aggressive stance and set its sights on Amritsar. Its invading force, consisting of the 1st Armoured Division and 11th Infantry Division, crossed the International Border and captured the Indian town of Khem Karan. The Indian Army needed urgent reinforcements, and the Tank division in Jhansi was called upon. That vital movement happened through Baroda. The then Collector was on casual leave, so I was in charge of the entire district. All passenger trains were cancelled and there were tanks thundering through Baroda all day and night. We deployed round the clock surveillance for vulnerable points along the route – one of which was the railway bridge on the River Vishwamitri which flows through the west of Baroda. The military, in fact, unearthed a plan to blow up the bridge and apprehended a spy as he was passing on messages to the Pakistan Army. I told the spy that he should be thankful that the Indian judicial system will still allow him a fair trial despite him being caught red-handed.

While the reinforcements arrived by 5 a.m., the Indian troops flooded the sugarcane fields near the village of Asal Uttar in the night. The next morning, the Pakistani tanks of the 1st Armoured Division were lured inside the trap. The swampy ground slowed down their advance and many of them could not move because of the muddy slush. Over 100 Pakistani tanks were destroyed and another 40 captured while India lost only 10 tanks during this counter-offensive. This battle is compared with the Battle of Kursk in the Second World War for how it changed the course of the India Pakistan war of 1965 in India's favour.

CHAPTER XVIII

Splattered

Assistant Collector, Baroda

My early days in Baroda involved a lot of travel across the district and I used to be on tour twenty days in a month. So if you take away the four Sundays as holidays, I was practically in the headquarters for only one day in the week. This was in line with the government order which mandated that cases be heard in the villages for the convenience of the people, rather than in the district headquarters. Now, the Assistant Collector, in those days used to have no vehicle allocated for official use. So I would typically take a bus in the morning with my peon Shivaji, carrying a huge bundle of files, in tow.

One such day, we boarded a state transport bus to Padra taluka. At Padra, we got on to another bus which would halt at the bus stop closest to our destination village. Beyond that, there were only dirt roads. Once we got off the bus, the 'talati' or revenue officer of the village, had arranged for a two-wheeled bullock cart as our pick up vehicle. We pulled up our trousers and got on to the wooden platform between the wheels, which was our not-so-comfortable seat for the ensuing forty-five minute ride to the village.

The 'talati' had chosen two of the finest bullocks to pull our cart guided by an enthusiastic charioteer. The charioteer, with a yoke hitched to the two bullocks on one hand and a thin whip on the other, was spurring on the rather healthy and robust animals. The cart gathered a brisk pace giving us a somewhat bumpy ride in the bargain, and we ended up off the seat for the most part. The bullocks must have been well fed so that they would have all the energy to sustain the one and a half hour journey from and to the village.

The feeding had a flip side which I, for one, had not anticipated. As hierarchy would have it, I was sitting ahead on the cart, with Shivaji behind me. Suddenly, the galloping bullocks at the top of their stride, eased themselves on me. In an epic moment, my entire face and the better part of my body was covered with dung. I had no spare clothes on me as the plan was to return home the same day. So there I was, with smelly dung splattered all over me and it progressively dried up as we rode on. When I reached the village, my condition was such that the 'talati' failed to recognise me. After some superficial cleaning, I addressed the issues in the village, and took the return route to Baroda in the evening. On the way back, Shivaji, offered many words of sympathy, repeating several times how unfair it was on the part of the government not to provide a vehicle to such a high ranking official.

CHAPTER XIX

An Almost-Costly Lunch

Assistant Collector, Baroda

At Baroda, I had joined as a supernumerary Assistant Collector, which is essentially a training stint before taking on independent responsibility, and I had no real work. The then Collector of Baroda, Mr Gangopadhyay, was very supportive and he used to say, "You are going to do the grind for the next thirty-five years anyway, so just relax and enjoy while you still can." Some days, I would come back home for lunch and then head back after a leisurely meal.

My neighbours, Mr Veen and his wife, were a very affectionate and friendly couple and Mr Veen, an officer at Sarabhai Chemicals, used to be home every day during lunch hour. It just happened that one particularly lazy week, I was home on three consecutive days and went over to their place for a tête-à-tête over lunch. We got lost in our conversations and both Mr Veen and I stretched our lunch hour before heading back to work.

A few days later, I saw that Mrs Veen seemed rather glum and tensed, so I asked her if all was well. She replied, "My husband has lost his job. He reached an hour late after lunch on three days the other week and they just asked him to leave, giving him three months' pay." I was shocked because I had known Mr Veen to be a very conscientious man.

I reached office early the following day and the first thing I did was to call up Mr Mukherjee, the then Managing Director at Sarabhai Chemicals. We had met at a couple of events and the Bengali connection had helped us build a quick rapport. I said, "Mr Mukherjee, do you treat your employees like slaves? Someone's late by an hour after lunch and you just sack him!" Mukherjee said that he had no clue about this case and if this was indeed the issue, he would have the person reinstated right away. I wrote a note that evening and handed it over to Mr Veen, requesting him to meet Mr Mukherjee. He had his job back.

Never did I talk at length with Mr Veen, thereafter, except on Sundays. There was no way I was going to risk another weekday conversation with him!

CHAPTER XX

An Honest Break

District Development Officer, Baroda

The nephew of the District Congress President was the contractor for lubrication of irrigation tube wells installed by the government. He used to divert some of the lubricating oil he got from the government for maintenance of tube wells, and sell it in the open market. When this came to my notice, I decided to prosecute him right away.

After intense lobbying by the District Congress President with the Chief Minister (CM) and the resulting pressure on the Chief Secretary (CS), the CS had a discussion with me. He told me that I had done the right thing and he was very appreciative of that fact. However, given the repeated appeals from the CM, he asked me if I would mind coming to 'Sachivalaya' – the Secretariat, on an important post. I replied that I was a bachelor and had just a bed and a suitcase to pick up, so it would be no problem. That's how I moved to the post of Deputy Secretary, Industries replacing an officer who was senior to me by seven years.

CHAPTER XXI

Lingua franca

Deputy Secretary, Industries
The Gujarat government had adopted the recommendations of the Parikh Committee to shift all official communication to the local language. But in the Industries department, we continued to make file notings in English since none of the department secretaries was too conversant in Gujarati.

Bhanjibhai Patel, the then Deputy Minister, was from Jamnagar and knew me since my days in the district. He called me over one day and said, "Samajpati, there is a government order that requires everyone to write in Gujarati. But you continue to comment in English. What do you think of yourself?" When I was back in the office and my Secretary, Mr Ghosh, enquired about the discussion, I narrated the conversation to him. Mr Ghosh said, "Is that how he spoke to you? From now on, don't send any file to the Deputy Minister, just mark it directly to the Minister."

After a couple of months, Bhanjibhai again called me and took objection to the fact that he was receiving no file from the Industries department. Upon hearing about the instruction from the Secretary, he complained to the then Chief Minister. The Chief Minister did not want to create a conflict and told him, with a hand on his shoulder that he, unfortunately, had two 'mathabhari' or headstrong Bengalis in the Industries department. It was best to just ignore them and not get into a confrontation. Instead, he could focus on other parts of his portfolio such as the 'Co-operatives department' which was 'very important' because it dealt with farmers' issues.

With this, the Deputy Minister was, for all practical purposes, divested of his Industries portfolio and no file pertaining to the department since went to him.

CHAPTER XXII

The Moral Fabric

Deputy Secretary, Industries

I was a Director and on the board of Digjam, an SK Birla group company into textiles. At one of the Annual Board Meetings, the company decided to present each Director with fabric of 1.2 metre length that could be suitably tailored. In those days, it was customary to maintain arm's length relationships with industrialists. Officers refrained from attending parties hosted by business people and accepting gifts of any nature was simply out of the question.

So even though the piece of cloth was of no significant material value, I declared it to the General Administration Department asking if it should be deposited with the government. Only when I received an approval for personal use, did I get a pair of trousers stitched.

CHAPTER XXIII

Bows and Arrows

Collector, Panchmahals

Panchmahals had been declared 'scarcity hit' due to poor rainfall that had created a drought-like situation across the district. We had initiated many public works projects to provide relief to the population and I was on a visit to Jhalod taluka, which had a significant Adivasi population, to review the relief operations there.

After a 100km drive from Godhra in my rickety Jeep, which made the journey seem even longer, I reached my destination. As I entered the taluka, in the distance I could see a large crowd. I went closer to investigate the matter and found a highly agitated mob. They were protesting about not having received their wages for the last fifteen days. Even as I was hearing them out, some of the tribals suddenly came menacingly towards me with their bows and arrows. I was totally cornered.

As luck would have it, a police party was coming from a prohibition raid at a nearby village just then. Seeing a large crowd and the collector's Jeep there, they sensed some tension. Around eight armed policemen rushed in to protect me just in the nick of time and I escaped a life-threatening situation with all limbs intact.

CHAPTER XXIV

Out of Order

Collector, Panchmahals

We had unexpected floods in Panchmahals, the first in almost fifty years! It was vital to have the phone lines working in order to coordinate all the rescue and relief operations. But at this critical juncture, we had massive connectivity failures and I found that the Sub Divisional Officer (SDO), Telephones was not responsive enough in trying to get the phone lines up and running.

This was an emergency situation and people's lives were in danger. I invoked MISA (Maintenance of Internal Security Act) and dictated the order for arresting the SDO and putting him behind bars for six months, due to the sustained disruption in communication services. But my personal assistant, out of the goodness of his heart, immediately informed the SDO of the order and he, in turn, rushed to meet me. He assured me of his best efforts and had connectivity restored in quick time. I did not need to sign the order.

CHAPTER XXV

Prohibition Raid on a Teetotaller

Collector, Panchmahals

My relationships with officers from other services in the district such as the police were always very cordial and friendly. PN Writer was the DIG, Baroda Range. A very upright and honest officer, he was in the army earlier and after WWII was absorbed in the IPS. Commonly known as 'Fighter Writer' because of his penchant for picking up spats especially with IAS officers, he had become a very good friend and would come over for a meal whenever he was in the city.

One day, I got an unexpected call at 4 a.m. from my executive engineer. He was panic-stricken because there had just been a prohibition raid at his house in the wee hours of the morning. I was rather surprised because I knew he did not drink and was sure there was something more here than met the eye. I told him I was entirely convinced of his innocence and asked him not to worry. Later that morning, I called the DSP (District Superintendent of Police) over and asked him to tell me what had happened.

Apparently, Writer had come on a tour to Godhra a few days before and was staying at the guest house, in the only room that had an air conditioner. A Deputy Minister happened to make an unplanned visit to the city at the same time. So this particular executive engineer, who was in charge of room allocations, requested Writer to move to another room, to which he took offence. He asked for the rule book that contains this directive. The engineer was in a quandary and sought my intervention. I called Writer up and asked him if he would vacate the room out of courtesy, which he did. But he bore a grudge against the engineer and asked the District Superintendent of Police (DSP) to 'fix' him.

After hearing the real story, I spoke to Writer and told him with a knowing smile, that I was aware of the truth behind the alcohol bottles at my engineer's residence. He didn't deny it and wanted to figure out instead who had spilled the beans. In friendly banter, I said that I had my sources, and asked him to have the case withdrawn and let my engineer off the hook. He obliged.

CHAPTER XXVI

A Poetic Exit

Collector, Panchmahals

Indira Gandhi was in the district for addressing a couple of public meetings. I was with the Prime Minister at the taluka where she had the first of her rallies. A message came in then, that there was an MP who had composed a poem in the PM's praise and wanted to recite it to the audience at Godhra, the venue of the next rally. Now from a security perspective, the protocol on who was to be on the dais was very clear – the PM, the Congress President and the Collector. I broke away from the convoy and reached Godhra fifteen minutes before the PM. The MP was up there on the dais. I directly went to him and requested him to step down urgently while explaining the security protocol. But he was very adamant, so I had to ask the police to forcibly evict him from the dais.

The MP complained to Indira Gandhi that he had been manhandled while he was only trying to sing her praises. She did not entertain the complaint and told him that the Collector, as District Magistrate, was in charge of the security of the Prime Minister, and had rightly done his duty.

CHAPTER XXVII

Ignoring Can Be Bliss

Collector, Panchmahals

During one of Indira Gandhi's visits to Godhra she was to stay overnight at the city Circuit House. Some opposition leaders had announced that they would be protesting, along with a large number of students, by banging 'thalis' i.e. plates at the Circuit House all night. This would have created a loud ruckus and I asked her, if we should have the protesters evicted since she had an early start the following morning. She said it would be best to allow them to go on with their plans and just ignore them. If they are forcibly removed they would then speak to the papers the following day and rake up the incident in the media. Instead, if their protest drew no attention, they would just get tired after an hour or two and head back home to sleep. And that is exactly what happened.

CHAPTER XXVIII

No Royal Privileges

Collector, Panchmahals

Baria State, founded in 1524, was one of the princely states of India during the period of the British Raj. More recently, it had become one of the talukas in Panchmahals and the Maharaja of Baria still used to stay there. I had a run-in with the king a couple of times.

The first time I visited the town, a messenger came to me saying that the Maharaja would like to meet me. While previous officials might have made courtesy calls on him, I did not want to recognise any extra-constitutional authority. I told the messenger that the Maharaja was free to meet me at the government guest house to discuss any problem pertaining to the people or himself, but if he expected me to go over to his residence for this, he was quite mistaken.

The second incident took place right after the abolition of privy purses. There was a directive that perks and privileges of erstwhile royal families, including possession of weapons beyond a permissible limit, were to be eliminated. I implemented that directive in toto and had all excess weapons collected from the Maharaja of Baria. He took strong offence and registered a complaint against me with the then Home Secretary. However, the complaint met with a quick closure since the actions taken were entirely in accordance with the law of the land.

CHAPTER XXIX

Without Fear or Favour

Deputy Secretary, Health

This is a story about a subordinate and a boss. My Joint Director, Family Planning was Dr Ambwani, an officer with a strong sense of integrity and effective at his work. But the then Health Secretary, my boss, bore a grudge against him. Apparently, they were both members of the reputed Ellisbridge Gymkhana in Ahmedabad before the Secretary assumed the current role, and would cross each other without exchanging pleasantries.

One day, my boss called me to say that I should keep a record of what time Dr Ambwani comes in, when he leaves, which days he comes late and so on. I replied that this was patently not my job and if she did want the details to be collected, she could perhaps ask her PA (Personal Assistant) to do it.

The next conflict came up when Dr Ambwani was due for promotion. I gave my assessment and recommended him for the next level. When the file reached my Health Secretary, she called me and was absolutely furious. She wanted to know how I could recommend such an officer for promotion. When I told her that in my assessment, the officer in question met all necessary criteria on performance and potential, she asked me to change my note. I refused to do that outright, telling her that it would be incongruous on my part to make a modification but as the Secretary, she had every right to overrule me.

My boss was in two minds but finally did override my recommendation. As per the rules of business, since the matter pertained to a Class I officer, the final authority for approving this promotion was the Chief Minister. The Chief Minister read the file with due attention and discerned a bias. I still remember the last paragraph of his comment on the file, "The assessment put up by the Secretary of the Health Department appears to be not objective in nature but subjective in character. I feel inclined to agree with the Deputy Secretary. Being the Chief Minister of the state, my assessment should prevail and the officer should be promoted." Dr Ambwani got his due.

CHAPTER XXX

Extraordinary Ordinance

Deputy Secretary, Health

Family Planning was the top priority of the Health Department, and we were doing quite well on the implementation front as a state. As part of the program, the government used to provide monetary incentives to people for adopting family planning measures. And sometimes when we fell short of funds, and disbursements were due, money used to be raised from other sources such as panchayats, to supplement available government resources. Dr Ghasura was the District Health Officer (DHO) in Kheda district. And he had raised some additional funds for incentive disbursement, upon my verbal instruction. While this was common practice, there was an existing order that without explicit permission, no government official could collect funds for any purpose. An enquiry was initiated against Dr Ghasura as an outcome of an audit exercise. He was deeply disturbed and feared that this would destroy his career.

While the order against the raising of supplementary resources did exist, I knew that the funds had been used for a pressing priority. I assured Dr. Ghasura of my unflinching support. I made a strong case and got the Panchayat Act amended through an Ordinance, which allowed for the raising of funds by a District Health Officer for family planning. My going out of the way and taking this unprecedented step to back my officer, gave a great impetus to the entire team and increased their trust in my leadership manifold.

CHAPTER XXXI

Disaster Doctor

Deputy Secretary, Health

As Deputy Secretary, I was assigned the charge of all the district hospitals and found that many positions for doctors, across the nineteen hospitals, were lying vacant. One of the malaises afflicting many organisations and so also the government is a general lack of ownership by the staff. Often times, employees just follow the process without being adequately concerned if the desired outcomes had been achieved. People before me must certainly have noticed the existing vacancies. They perhaps even put out advertisements for the same. But that's where they would have halted their effort and not bothered to close the loop. With a little bit of rigour, I was able to get all the vacancies filled with qualified doctors through a mix of internal movements and fresh hiring.

There is a district called Dangs which has a large tribal population. Amarsinh Chaudhary was a tribal leader and a Minister at that time. One day, he asked me, "Samajpati, are you against tribals?" I was taken aback by the question and asked him why he said so. He replied that the civil surgeon who had moved to Dangs was giving many people lifelong injuries through his skill with the scalpel, or his lack thereof. I immediately enquired into the facts and gathered that while the doctor was quite senior, his record with surgeries was indeed very dismal. After having his academic record verified, and speaking to the medical college he graduated from, I figured that he had failed five times in his academics. Finally, he had pleaded with the

Medical College for lenient marking, promising never to undertake a surgery as a doctor. But he joined the government, and with time the history of his many failed attempts was erased.

I moved him out of the role of civil surgeon immediately and placed him in an administrative role.

CHAPTER XXXII

Expressing Opinion

When Babubhai Jashbhai Patel was the Chief Minister, he once appointed a working group called the 'Parikh Committee', which recommended that all notings on files should be in the local language. Many of my colleagues moved to writing either short comments or just signing on the note drafted by their subordinates. I did not.

Once Babubhai Jashbhai called me and said with some displeasure, "Samajpati, you are aware of the Parikh Committee report. But what is this? You still write everything in English!" I said, "Sir, to be frank with you, if you want my opinion it would need to be in English because I am, unfortunately, not able to express myself well in Gujarati. If you want my clerk's advice, on the other hand, we can move to Gujarati." He immediately said, "No, no, no! You can continue writing in English."

CHAPTER XXXIII

The Height of Pettiness

Honest officers come in the way of people with motives and the problem is that because they have a clean record, it's difficult to find skeletons in the cupboard. However, there were a few bizarre allegations that were typically used against such officers.

The first was the 'patawala' or peon enquiry. As a Collector in the district, it was common practice to have a peon or man Friday at the residence for day jobs like handling official visitors, picking up calls and so on. While there was no official sanction for this, it was very much the norm. Once when I was Secretary, Panchayats there was an application against one of my junior officers, Takru, an impeccable bureaucrat, that he had two peons doing day jobs at his residence. And Takru was not one for hiding anything, so he had even admitted that he did have peons at home. I received the file where my Deputy Secretary had gone to great lengths to note how this was a misuse of government resources for personal benefit. After my comments, the file was due to go the Secretary, Personnel in the General Administration Department, who I knew was quite a sadist and would harass Takru further. I just put my comments on the file and held it back till that particular Secretary got transferred.

The second kind of enquiry was even more ridiculous. The newspapers at an officer's residence used to be paid for by the government, and the policy was that at the end of the month, the 'pasti' or old newspapers were to be handed over to the office. The absence of a few newspapers, which might have gone into some household use, used to be the subject of another set of flimsy enquiries. When I was Deputy Secretary, Industry, Power and Mines, I received a complaint that my Director of Mines had not deposited back old newspapers and accordingly an enquiry had been initiated. As per due procedure, I mentioned this to the Secretary of the Department. We were both aghast at the frivolousness of the complaint, for it reflected the utter baseness of the complainant than anything else. The complaint was shelved right away.

CHAPTER XXXIV

Neighbour's Envy

The 1980s was not just the pre-internet era, it was the pre-cable TV era. There were no dish antennas to collect powerful digital signals from satellites, but we had the humble rooftop aerials, which used to try to latch on to feeble signals being sent by the TV Towers. A new TV station had come up in Ahmedabad and all of us were trying to identify the 'perfect' angle for our aerial to catch the signal. My morning ritual would include climbing on to the terrace top to rotate the aerial and I would find all my neighbours up on their terraces too, struggling with the same challenge. We would look at each other's aerials to figure out if someone had discovered the 'magic' direction.

One of my colleagues and neighbours, who was the then Secretary, Personnel, called me one day to ask how my television reception was. This, given the above context, was a very common occurrence and I told him that the reception had been pretty good of late, especially since I had bought my new Sony TV. He said he would like to come over on the Sunday and check it out, and so he did. We had some tea and snacks and chatted for half an hour with the discussion largely centred around the extent of 'snowing' on the television and the latest hacks to reduce it.

To my utter astonishment, on the Monday, I got a letter from the same Secretary, Personnel asking for an explanation regarding the Sony TV in my house – the source of funding for a 'Japanese' television, customs duty paid receipts in case it was imported and similar queries. It was a long letter with almost ten points on which I was supposed to revert. I was quite amazed to see the pettiness of it all and thought that the letter did not even merit a reply. I asked my PA to just file the document. I received many diligent reminders over the next few months but never bothered to respond. Meanwhile, the Secretary Personnel was transferred and the new officer had his priorities better sorted. I stopped getting the reminders.

CHAPTER XXXV

Knowledge is Power

Whenever I joined a new assignment, I used to avidly read everything related to the department – law books, expert articles, past practices, regulations - everything that would give me a deep domain understanding. I always found that this was an important source of my contribution and effectiveness and earned me the respect of my team. Unless you know the department in and out, you will always be dependent on your subordinates' view point which might not always be correct or unbiased. When you have thorough knowledge you can take decisions powered by your own thinking. While in the Forest Department, I delved deep into sustainability and the ecology on the one hand, and environment policies and laws on the other.

I authored several independent papers accepted at international fora, without assistance from any expert. I remember the last one was on the Eucalyptus tree and how it affects soil fertility. I was to present it at an international symposium, but was transferred just then. My successor read out the paper on my behalf at the seminar.

I also used to be well-versed with the laws and bye-laws pertaining to the department. On one instance, I dictated the Saurashtra Tree Felling Act, in its entirety, to create a relevant framework for protecting tree plantations and conserving forests. The then Legal Secretary, Bhatt, who later went on to become the Chief Justice of two High Courts in the country, was quite taken aback at my comprehensive draft, since the norm was for the Legal department to prepare such documents.

CHAPTER XXXVI

In the Balance

81

I started my career in the civil services, with a monthly salary of Rs. 400, and having incurred expenditure on the construction of my house and the wedding of my elder child, I retired with a bank balance of Rs. 127 which incidentally is also my house number. Sometimes I wonder if only my house number had a few more digits to it perhaps so would my bank balance at retirement.

About The Author

Chittaranjan Samajpati

Mr Chittaranjan (C.R.) Samajpati is an IAS officer of the batch of 1962.

Born in Greater Bengal, Chitta, as he was fondly called, was the youngest of three siblings. With his many cousins and pampering aunts and uncles living just a stone's throw away, the family, though, always felt much larger. Childhood was thus a period of endless mirth and play in the company of friends and kinfolk. And when he was not playing, Chitta was deep into books.

Everything changed with Partition. Chitta faced a painful uprooting from his homeland, having to flee with his mother, elder brother and sister in the dead of night leaving everything behind, with his father incarcerated due to political persecution.

As refugees in an unknown place, the family had little to fall back on and had to rebuild everything bit by bit. The difficult times, however, helped Chitta develop a formidable ability to stay resolute in the face of adversity and this would serve him well in later years. He remained focussed on his academics, accomplishing his BA Honours and then his MA in Economics from Calcutta University.

Mr Samajpati joined the IAS and was assigned to the Gujarat cadre. He served at the top levels of administration across a diverse set of assignments, retiring as Additional Chief Secretary, Govt. of Gujarat. During his over three decades in public service, his work meant everything to him. He was tough on himself and demanding of his subordinates. And he did not allow anything to come in the way - not the system's inertia, not self-seeking politicians, not vested business interests. This led, at times, to his paying a high personal price but also resulted in his being able to create exceptional impact and social good.

Mr Samajpati finally met his match in his three grandchildren whom he adoringly gives in to more often than not.

www.ingramcontent.com/pod-product-compliance
Lightning Source LLC
Chambersburg PA
CBHW020453160726
47991CB00007B/2635